The Mystery of Robin Hood: Fact or Fantasy?

By
Tom Lisker

Illustrated by
Samuel B. Whitehead

cpi
contemporary perspectives, inc.

Copyright© 1979 by Contemporary Perspectives, Inc.
All rights reserved. No part of this book may be reproduced or utilized in any form or
by any means, electronic or mechanical, or by any information storage and retrieval
system, without permission in writing from the Publisher. Inquiries should be
addressed to the PUBLISHER: Contemporary Perspectives, Inc., 223 East 48th
Street, New York, New York 10017.

This book is distributed by Silver Burdett Company, Morristown, New Jersey 07960.

Library of Congress Number: 79-18396

Every effort has been made to trace the ownership of all copyrighted material in this
book and to obtain permission for its use.

Library of Congress Cataloging in Publication Data

Lisker, Tom, 1928 —
  The mystery of Robin Hood.

  SUMMARY: Retellings of some of the tales about
Robin Hood interspersed with evidence and speculation
concerning whether or not he ever really existed.
    1. Robin Hood — Legends. [1. Robin Hood. 2.
Folklore — England] I. Title.
PZ8.1.L68My   398.2'2'0941   79-18396
ISBN 0-89547-079-9

Manufactured in the United States of America
ISBN 0-89547-079-9

Contents

Chapter 1

A Hungry Man
Turns Outlaw

Slowly ... very slowly, the young man pulled back on his bow. A lone deer moved in and out of the forest's deep shadows. One moment the animal could be seen. The next moment it was hidden. There was nothing the young man could do but wait.

Robert Fitzooth was the young man's name. He was not a hunter. But he had not eaten a full meal for days. The year 1100 had been a bad one for English farmers. The weather was not good and the crops had failed. Poor people everywhere were hungry. If that deer would step out into the light, Robert would eat his first real meal in days.

The deer stopped at a patch of sunlit grass. Robert stood frozen in the clearing. He knew he was the finest shot in the land. Still, the deer was so far away he could not be sure. It took most of Robert's strength just to aim and steady his bow. Would his arrow fly far enough? He raised his bow and shot the arrow. Whap! The deer fell.

"At last!" Robert cried. "A real meal! But who will believe such a shot? Only I was here to see it!"

Young Robert was wrong. A group of the king's foresters had seen it all. They were hidden among the trees near the fallen animal. As Robert reached down for his deer, he heard someone come up behind him.

"You there — marksman," a voice called. "Halt by order of the king! Put down your weapons!"

Robert turned to find a captain of the king's forest police glaring at him. Terror filled Robert's heart as he watched the rest of the king's policemen move in to surround him.

"Good evening, my lord," Robert called out. He greeted the captain as cheerfully as he could. "How may I serve you, kind sir?"

"Serve *me*?" the captain laughed. "You can serve me in only one way, young man. Obey the law. A deer lies dead at your feet!" shouted the captain. "By what right did you kill the king's deer? We *saw* you kill it!"

And then the captain added, "Too bad such skill as yours will be wasted. Death is the price people pay for killing one of the king's deer."

"*Wasted*, my lord?" Robert raised his arms in doubt. "I am only a simple fellow. There is much in life I do not understand. Surely all men have the right to eat. These are hard times, my lord."

Quietly Robert dropped his arms and slipped an arrow to his bow. The captain moved toward him.

"All men may eat," the captain said, "but none may kill the king's deer. This animal did not belong to you. I'm afraid its death will cost you your life." The captain then signaled his men. "Arrest this man at once!"

Robert jumped back. He raised his bow and pointed it at the captain.

"Stand back, good sirs." Robert took a final look at his deer. "I have never wronged my king. Surely he does not wish his subjects to starve. Tell him of our troubles — and I know he will excuse me."

The captain raised his sword. But as soon as he did, an arrow from Robert's bow passed through his arm. Amazed, the captain and his men froze in their tracks.

"Farewell, my lord," yelled Robert as he ran off into the forest and quickly disappeared.

From that day on Robert Fitzooth would spend his life in those woods. A hunted man, he would hide among the tallest trees of the forest. He would change his name. His mother had always called him Robin.

And to that nickname he would add the name "Hood," for the hood he would wear to hide his face.

For many years the people of England told stories about Robin Hood, the famous outlaw of the forest. Their tales described Robin and a group of men like him who had banded together to hide from the king's police. All were strong, brave, trustworthy, and loyal to one another. And all were happy to have found each other — they were "Robin Hood and his band of merry men."

Although they were outlaws, to most people they were heroes. Robin and his merry men stole only from the rich. They shared what they stole with England's poor.

Robin himself was the gentlest of thieves. He never sent away those he robbed without food or water. He tried never to harm anyone. The stories of Robin and his merry men are perhaps the most famous outlaw stories in history. Yet even today, no one knows whether or not the stories about them are true.

Was Robin Hood, born Robert Fitzooth, a real person? Or did Robin Hood — outlaw of the forest — come from the mind of some storyteller? In the pages that follow, we will try to find the truth. Together we will explore ... The Mystery of Robin Hood.

Chapter 2
The Mystery of Robin Hood

There is no real record of Robin Hood in history — certainly nothing anyone can rely on to prove there ever was such a person. In fact, not much at all was written about him during the time he was said to have lived. It was not until 200 years later, around the year 1300, that a Robin Hood adventure was put down on paper.

The earliest Robin Hood stories were passed along from one person to another through *ballads*. A ballad is a song that tells a story. Hundreds of years ago *minstrels* (traveling actors and singers) brought these songs from place to place all over England. The people of each town would gather by their fires to listen to the minstrels' ballads. This was how news of the day traveled.

These ballads of Robin Hood were always popular. The stories were told again and again through each passing generation. But in 200 years storytellers might have made up a lot about Robin Hood that was not true. Their tales might have become more exciting each

time they were told. This often happens when stories are passed from one person to another. Heroes become stronger and braver. The people they fight become more evil and cruel. But even if the tales of Robin Hood changed, there are many people today who think that such a person may have lived.

Still, there are so many tales about Robin Hood it is hard to believe one person could have lived through so many adventures. Some historians think this can be explained. Perhaps there was more than one hero for the common people. Perhaps there were many heroes who had many adventures. Over the years all of these stories and all of these heroes were put together. If so, "Robin Hood" simply became the one name used by storytellers for all these exciting people.

For example, there are different stories told to explain why Robin became an outlaw. One says that his father, William Fitzooth, was the king's head forester in Nottingham, England. One day the sheriff of Nottingham sent William to prison even though the man had done nothing wrong. His son, Robin, became an outlaw to get even with the mean sheriff.

Another story says that Robin was a wild young man. After spending all his money he found he could no longer pay his bills. Afraid he would be arrested, Robin ran away and hid in the northern forest lands. Here he gathered 100 of the best archers in the land.

Together they spent their lives stealing from the rich and helping the poor.

Whatever one chooses to believe, there is still another difficult question to answer about Robin Hood. If there really was a Robin Hood, when did he live?

Some tales say Robin lived during the time of King Henry II. This was about the year 1160. But others say he lived some 200 years later, in the 1300s. This would have been in the time of King Edward II.

Of course, there are probably many people today who believe Robin Hood is only a legend, a made-up story. These people point to the tales of how Robin met each of the "merry men." All the stories seem so much alike. How can they be true? If minstrels wrote and rewrote their ballads, the true stories must have changed over the years.

The stories that tell how Robin Hood met two of the more famous "merry men" — Little John and Friar Tuck — are good examples of how the minstrels may have "helped" make the real facts a little more interesting.

Chapter 3

How Robin Hood Met the Merry Men

The Story of Little John

One summer day Robin Hood came upon a stream in the middle of Sherwood Forest. Although the stream was not deep, Robin did not want to get his feet wet. He decided to walk further down the bank to a narrow footbridge.

As Robin walked he saw a very large man on the other side of the stream. This man seemed to be heading for the same crossing. Neither man said a word. But each began to step more quickly. Soon it was clear that both were going to try crossing the bridge at the same time. But the little bridge was wide enough for only one of them at a time.

Robin reached for his sword. Then he saw that the other man carried no weapon. All he had with him was a long wooden pole. The two men reached the bridge at exactly the same moment.

"You there!" the man shouted to Robin. "Wait for me to cross. I'm in a hurry!"

Before the other man could take another step, Robin jumped a few feet ahead. Both men now stood on the bridge facing each other.

The man crashed his pole against the bridge. The narrow bridge shook from one end to the other. The two angry men walked toward each other. As they got close Robin realized that he was looking at the largest person he had ever seen!

"Now there, little fellow," the man said calmly. "Do you turn around and get out of my way, or do I throw you over the side?"

"My, you are either very brave — or very foolish, sir," Robin replied. "Can't you see my sword?"

Suddenly Robin felt the end of a wooden pole against his chest.

"If you would use a sword against an unarmed man then go ahead," said the man. "But I will not move, sir, until you're out of my way."

Robin was angry. Still, he liked the man's courage. Here was someone willing to fight for what he thought was right. That gave Robin an idea.

"All right, sir, there's only one thing to do. Wait here and I will get myself a pole. Then we can decide this like men."

Robin returned to the forest and cut a branch to use as a pole. All the while the big man was laughing. It was clear that he liked Robin as much as Robin liked him.

"Say a prayer, young sir," the man shouted. "It's a bit of a fall from the bridge."

"I'll say a prayer. But it will be for *you*, big fellow."

And with that Robin swung at the man. But his pole was short of the target. Robin tried again, and then again. Each time the larger man proved faster. Finally Robin felt his pole lifted from his hands. It splashed into the water below. The big man smiled.

"Farewell," the man called to Robin. "I'm afraid I must be moving on. Will you allow me to cross first?"

Before Robin could answer he found himself flying over the railing and into the water below. As he gathered himself together, Robin heard a roar from above. The big fellow was laughing as hard as he could.

Robin had to laugh himself. He knew he looked pretty funny sitting there in two feet of water. When he got back to the bank, the other man was there to help. He wore a huge smile.

The big man laughed as he stretched out his hand to Robin. But suddenly his laughter stopped. As soon as

Robin had grasped his arm, he pulled the man forward. Together the two fell back into the water.

The man jumped up, ready to fight. But when he saw Robin laughing, he calmed down. Soon both men were laughing so hard that their sides hurt.

"What's your name?" Robin asked when he had caught his breath.

"John Little, good sir."

"Well then, 'Little John,' we seem to be much alike. Join me, if you like, and make a friend for life."

Little John and Robin shook hands right there in the middle of the stream. And from that day forward the two men were close friends.

The Story of Friar Tuck

One day Robin Hood and his merry men were practicing with bows and arrows. Little John had just gotten off an excellent shot.

"Little John," laughed Robin, "in all the world there is only one who can shoot better than you."

"And who may that be?" Little John asked.

"Of course you know," Robin said with some surprise. "*I* am the best shot in the land."

Little John was about to answer when Will Scarlet broke in.

"Not so fast, gentlemen," Will said. "I've heard there's one good enough to beat the two of you! He's Friar Tuck of Fountain's Abbey."

While the others argued that it couldn't be so, Robin began to pack his things. "Let's find him then and see if it's true." And together with Little John, Will, and several of the others, Robin headed off in search of Friar Tuck. They followed a path close to the river that wound its way to the abbey.

The small band had just passed the final bend in the river. The abbey was just around the other side.

Robin signaled the others to wait. He would go on alone. He had gone only a little further when he heard voices coming from across the river. Two men seemed to be sharing dinner.

"Help yourself, lad," one voice said.

"No, you first please," said the other. "Have some meat pudding."

"Why, thank you, my lord," replied the first.

The two voices sounded very much alike to Robin. A close look told him why. One man — a big, round-faced, round-bellied friar — was talking to himself! In front of him was a huge platter of food. Robin never dreamed one man could eat so much. The friar was scooping meat and pies to his mouth with both hands.

"Say, friar," Robin yelled across the river, "I'd like some of that food before you eat it all."

"And how do you suppose you're going to get it, young fellow?" asked the surprised friar, seeing a young stranger across the water. Not only was the young man rude enough to spy on him, but his bow held an arrow that was pointed right at the friar.

"Why, you're going to come across the river and carry me back — that's how," called Robin, holding tightly to his bow.

The fat friar really didn't have much choice. Robin's arrow was aimed right at his stomach. Besides, Robin looked serious. The friar lifted his robes and waded across the narrow river. There he bent over, and a smiling Robin jumped on his back.

Robin laughed merrily as he rode piggyback across the river. But there was a twinkle in the friar's eye he could not see. When they reached the middle of the

river, the friar suddenly straightened up and threw Robin into the air. Robin's bow went flying as he landed in the cold water.

Now it was the friar's turn to laugh. But Robin saw nothing funny about this turn of events. He drew his sword. "Friar," he called, "draw your sword." They fought hard and long through the whole afternoon. Robin was a fine swordsman, but so was the friar. Finally, tired from the battle, Robin held up his hand.

"Whoa," he said. "Let us rest, good friar. And will you permit me just one thing? A blow on my horn?"

"Do as you wish, lad," puffed the friar, for he was tired and out of breath. "Blow till your eyes fall out."

Robin put his silver horn to his lips and blew three blasts. In an instant Little John, Will Scarlet, and two more of the merry men were there. The friar was stunned to see that Robin had help so close by.

"Since I let you blow your horn, good sir, might I have a whistle or two?" the friar asked Robin.

"Whistle till your ears pop," Robin answered.

Before the friar had finished three whistles, 100 dogs came bounding through the woods. The dogs

headed straight for Robin and his men. The men shot
arrow after arrow, but the dogs actually caught most of
the arrows safely with their *mouths*!

Robin and all the others ran for the cover of
low-hanging trees. All, that is, except Will Scarlet. He
was beside himself with laughter at the sight of Robin
hanging from a tree.

24

"Call off your dogs, Friar Tuck," Will called.

"Friar Tuck!" Robin called in amazement. "You are Friar Tuck? I am Robin Hood."

Friar Tuck was equally amazed. "*You* are Robin Hood? If I'd known that, you could have shared my food. I have heard good things about you."

"Good friar," Robin said, "you are as stout a fighter as you are a man. Won't you come to Sherwood Forest and join our happy band? You can be our friar and help those who are in need."

"Join you I will," said Friar Tuck. "For your cause is good and is the same as my own sworn duty."

The friar, Robin, and the merry men all returned to the camp in Sherwood Forest — with 100 dogs barking happily at their heels.

※

How alike are these stories? In both Robin challenges the strength and character of men he happens to meet. When he finds they are as fair and honest as he, Robin asks the men to join his band. Both Little John and Friar Tuck willingly agree. After their battles with Robin they can see that Robin is a man to respect. His ideas are worth fighting for.

Chapter 4

How Robin Hood Tricked the Sheriff of Nottingham

In old England the people's favorite Robin Hood stories were the ones in which Robin tricked the sheriff of Nottingham. Of course, we don't know if any of these stories are really true. But we are certain there *was* a real sheriff of Nottingham.

In many tales the sheriff of Nottingham was Robin's greatest enemy. No sheriff was a popular person in those days. After all, it was the sheriff who collected land taxes and enforced the laws. But the sheriff of Nottingham was not simply disliked; he was hated. Nowhere in England, it was said, was there a sheriff so cruel.

As you read this tale, remember that to some it may have really happened. To others it is only a story about what people of the time might have *wished* would happen.

Early one morning things were quiet in Sherwood Forest. As always, Robin was busy thinking of new ways to trap the sheriff of Nottingham. Robin especially liked tricks that showed others how cruel and greedy the sheriff really was.

During a morning walk through the forest, Robin met a hard-working butcher from a small town nearby.

"Good morning, butcher," said Robin. "How much for your cart, your meat, and your butcher's robe?"

"Are you serious, sir?" asked the butcher.

"I couldn't be more serious. How much?"

Robin, of course, paid the butcher a little more than he had asked. Then, disguised as the butcher, Robin Hood headed for Nottingham. There he set up his cart with all the other butchers.

Robin had a strange way of selling his meat. He sang a pleasant little song that told the shoppers he would sell three pennies worth of meat for only one penny and a kiss from the ladies. Never had the people of Nottingham heard of such a butcher. While the other meat sellers may not have been happy with Robin Hood, the townspeople were delighted with him.

It wasn't long before Robin was receiving lots of kisses from his customers. And it wasn't long before he had run out of meat. At first, the other butchers

thought he was a thief. But what thief gives away what he steals? They thought this must be the crazy son of some rich landowner.

Robin knew that this would be one of the days when the sheriff would ask all of Nottingham's food merchants to feast with him at the town hall. This was the way the sheriff made sure of getting the best foods for his own meals. Robin gladly accepted the sheriff's invitation.

Word of the strange butcher who had given away meat had already reached the sheriff of Nottingham. Like the others, the sheriff thought Robin was some rich and crazy young man. Perhaps he himself could trick this strange butcher out of some money.

"Sit by me," said the sheriff as Robin Hood passed his table. Robin, of course, was glad to sit with him.

The two men talked and laughed through the meal. Then Robin Hood, still playing the part of the strange butcher, surprised everyone in the room with a short speech. He suddenly climbed up on one of the tables and announced that he was going to pay for the feast.

The sheriff was delighted. The butcher's generosity meant that *he* would have to pay nothing. He leaned toward Robin. "You are a right merry soul," he said. "You must have a lot of money to spend it so freely."

"Oh, that I have, good sheriff," answered Robin. "But I have much more than money. I have brothers, and I own lots of land and many cattle."

"How much land do you and your brothers have?" the sheriff wanted to know.

"I don't know if we ever figured it out. There's plenty, though, believe me." At this point Robin leaned over and whispered so only the sheriff could hear. "But just between you and me — my brothers and I would rather have money than land and cattle."

At this news the sheriff became so excited that he could barely stay in his chair. "How much money would you want for all your land and cattle?" he asked.

"Oh, more than anyone has ever been able to afford," answered Robin with a sigh. "I think, though, that someone could buy it all for 500 pieces of gold."

Five hundred gold pieces was a fortune for most people in Nottingham. But the sheriff of Nottingham was no ordinary person. He had cheated the local people out of thousands of pieces of gold.

"I'll tell you what I'll do," said the sheriff. "I'll give you 300 pieces for it all. Can we settle everything tonight?"

"Sheriff, the land is worth a lot more," Robin began. He smiled brightly, knowing the greedy sheriff had taken the bait. "But since you are such a *good* and *kind* man, I will take your offer."

The sheriff jumped from his chair. How easily he had tricked this foolish young man! It was not the first

time he had taken advantage of someone. But this time might prove to be of greater value.

The next morning Robin signed papers selling the land and cattle to the sheriff. Then they set off to find the sheriff's new land and cattle. The sheriff carried along the 300 pieces of gold he promised to pay.

Robin led the sheriff deeper and deeper into Sherwood Forest. Finally they stopped before a herd of wild deer.

"These are my cattle, dear sir," laughed Robin, "and here are my brothers." At that Robin's merry men ran out from the forest, quickly surrounding the sheriff. The sheriff was stunned. He was trapped.

"Don't feel too bad, sheriff," Robin teased. "But learn this lesson. Your greed was just too strong for your head. Now, come join us for a grand dinner. There will be meat, pies, music, and games. You may as well enjoy yourself! Tonight's feast will cost you exactly 300 pieces of gold!"

We will never know if Robin Hood ever really tricked the greedy sheriff of Nottingham. But such tales have been told for hundreds of years. So true or not, people have found an idea in this story important enough to keep repeating.

Chapter 5

Robin Hood and
Sir Richard of Lea

In every adventure that has been written, Robin
Hood is fair to those who are honest. He deals harshly
only with those who take advantage of others. Robin
never seems to care about his own wealth or comfort.
Even today, he is thought of as a man who stole only
from the rich so he could give to the poor.

The most important thing to Robin Hood was that a
man or woman be honest and fair to others. If you did
all you could to treat your neighbors fairly, Robin
would do all he could to help you, rich *or* poor.

Late one spring morning Robin Hood is said to have
stopped a knight who was traveling through the forest.
The knight's name was Sir Richard of Lea. If Sir
Richard had had any riches not rightly his, Robin
surely would have taken them. But Sir Richard soon
found he had nothing to fear. Robin Hood found him
to be a good and honest man. The two became friends.

Robin learned that Sir Richard was about to lose
everything he had in the world. The year before, his

son had entered the jousting matches. He had fought the strongest knights in England. All had gone well until the last ride of the day. His lance broke, and a splinter sliced through the other rider's helmet. A few minutes later the other man died of the wound.

It had been an accident, but other knights, jealous of Sir Richard's son, said he had cheated. If they could not beat the young knight fairly, they would have him branded a cheat and a murderer. Sir Richard's son wanted to give money to the dead knight's family. His father borrowed several bags of gold to give to them. When he gave them the money, Sir Richard begged them to believe that his son was no murderer. The family believed it had been an accident. They would not ask for revenge.

But this was not the end of Sir Richard's troubles. The man who had loaned him the money — Sir Guy of Hereford — had at first said he would not need the money until Sir Richard was able to sell some land. But now Sir Guy wanted his money back right away. He was holding a note for the money that Sir Richard had signed without reading it carefully. If he wasn't paid within a month, Sir Guy would take away all of Sir Richard's lands.

Robin Hood felt sorry for Sir Richard. He knew the man had done nothing more than try to protect his innocent son. Robin Hood also knew how Sir Guy had

made most of his money. He loaned money at high rates no one could afford. He charged his tenants too much for the small farms they rented from him. Sir Richard was not the first to be cheated by this evil man. Nor, Robin Hood knew, would he be the last. But there must be some way to get back at Sir Guy — to punish him for what he stole from others.

Robin Hood made a plan. He sent Sir Guy an invitation to a party at the home of one of the most important Nottingham families. Little John delivered the note and drove the carriage that had been sent to bring Sir Guy through the forest.

Little John *did* bring Sir Guy to a party that night. But it was a party in the forest. The host was Robin Hood. And Sir Guy paid for all the food and wine. He also paid the debts he had forced on the people he cheated. When Sir Guy went home that night, his bags had none of the gold he always carried with him.

Some of Sir Guy's gold was given to the people who worked on his lands and owed him too much money to ever leave. Sir Richard took the money he needed only upon his promise that he would repay it as a loan.

◀ To prove their strength, knights fought in jousting matches.

⊰❘ Chapter 6 ❘⊱

Robin Hood and Good King Richard

Robin Hood's fame had spread across England. Even King Richard, called "Richard the Lion-Hearted," had heard of him. One day the king himself set out to capture the outlaw of Sherwood Forest.

King Richard and six of his finest, bravest knights put on priests' robes and headed for the woods. The king knew that once in the forest, he would not need to look for Robin Hood. The famous outlaw would find *him*. And right he was.

"Whoa, holy brothers," Robin called as he stepped out onto the road before them. "Have you a few extra gold coins to share with a poor man of the woods?"

King Richard looked closely at the woodsman before him. He knew right away that this was Robin Hood. "Please do not hurt us, sir," the disguised king said. "And do not touch our robes. We've sworn not to show our faces for 24 hours."

"Fair enough," said Robin. "I will not make you break a vow. But let me take your purses while you

join us for ..." Robin counted out half the coins, "... a 50-gold-piece dinner you won't soon forget." Quickly he put the 50 gold pieces into his pocket and returned 50 to the priests.

Then Robin and his men took the king's party back to the camp for the dinner they had just "bought." After a great meal, Robin rose and offered a toast.

"Here's to good King Richard. Long live the king!"

Along with all the others, King Richard joined in Robin's toast. "Why would outlaws like you drink to the health of the king?" he then asked. "Do you think of yourselves as loyal subjects?"

"We are indeed, sir," Robin answered proudly. "We would give our lives for him — and for his good cause. Ah, but why do we get so serious after such a wonderful meal? Will Scarlet, let us show the good friars how we play our games!"

The king kept watching this man they called Robin Hood. *Whatever the man is,* thought the king, *he is not just another outlaw! Could Robin Hood ever be made to leave this forest life to join the royal army?*

The king's thoughts came to a sudden halt. Robin's voice rose over the nighttime sounds of the forest.

"Each of you will shoot three arrows at this target," Robin told his men. "If any of you miss the center, it will cost you a blow from Will Scarlet's right hand."

The shooting began at once. Even the king was surprised at how well Robin Hood's band handled their bows. Only a few of the men missed the center of the target, and Will Scarlet sent those who missed sprawling with one whack from his strong arm.

When Robin's turn arrived, he ordered that the target be set even further away. Aiming carefully and with a steady pull on the bow, his first two arrows struck the very center of the target. But on his third shot, Robin's arrow missed the mark by a hair. Everyone laughed harder than ever. The king wondered if even the great Robin Hood was man enough to allow Will Scarlet to knock him down.

"Go to it, Will!" shouted Friar Tuck. "Give Robin the hardest blow of all."

"Hold on," said Robin. "I am king here, and no subject may strike the king. But even as our good King Richard would obey a holy order, I will obey these holy men who are our guests. Good friars, I leave my punishment in your holy hands. And if any of you can make me fall to the ground, I'll give you back your gold."

"I . . . I will try, sir!" said King Richard in the meekest voice he could manage. He rolled up his sleeve. Robin, who had been smiling, looked at the friar's arm. *A friar with muscles as big as my own*, he thought. King Richard gave Robin a punch the likes of which the outlaw had never felt before. Robin went sprawling to the dust. He lay there, red-faced, while the laughter of the merry men echoed all through Sherwood Forest. Robin was angry. But he was true to his word. He told Will Scarlet to return the gold.

Just then Sir Richard of Lea burst into the clearing. "Robin, Robin," he called. "I just heard that the king himself is searching for you. You must leave Sherwood Forest. Go to my castle and hide there."

Only when he had finished speaking did Sir Richard look at Robin's seven dinner guests. "Who are they?" he asked. As he looked at the men in the priests' robes, the color rose in Sir Richard's cheeks. He recognized the king! Sir Richard leaped from his horse and fell to his knees at once.

"How dare you offer your castle for this outlaw to hide?" asked the king sternly. "Why would you, a good and loyal knight, protect this outlaw from me?"

Sir Richard looked up at his king. "I am sorry, Your Majesty," he said, "but I owe my life to Robin Hood. It is only right that I help him."

King Richard smiled. "Rise my good man. I understand what you are saying. I have seen for myself that Robin Hood is a fine man. I do not say that all he has done is right. But I pardon him and all his men."

"Robin," the king asked, "will you join my service? I would be honored if you would return to London with me." A great roar went up, until all of Sherwood Forest was filled with the sound of cheering.

When Robin Hood said farewell to his men, he promised to return to them shortly. He could not know, at that time, that it would be years before he saw any of them again.

The former outlaw of Sherwood Forest was knighted for his service to the king and was given the title Earl of Huntington.

He journeyed on a great crusade to the Holy Lands. There the king and Robin fought side by side through many a bitter and bloody battle.

In the end the good, brave King Richard was killed. King Richard's men marched into an enemy trap. Outnumbered fifty to one, they fought well and bravely. As the battle was ending the king was struck down by an arrow. England's lion-hearted king was dead. Robin Hood was also wounded during that fight.

Legend has it that although in great pain, Robin Hood lived long enough to return to his beloved England. There he spoke with his dear friend, Little John, one last time. Knowing he had little time left, Robin asked Little John to take him to the castle of Sir Richard of Lea.

"My dear Little John," whispered Robin when they arrived. "Hand me my bow and choose the straightest arrow from your quiver."

Sadly, Little John did as his friend and leader asked. With his last bit of strength, Robin shot the arrow through a window.

"Where the arrow lands, Little John, let them dig my grave. And see to it that it will always be as green as the trees of Sherwood Forest."

And so, say the stories, Robin Hood died. When he was buried, a stone was set to mark the grave. On it were these words:

Here underneath this little stone
Lies Robert, Earl of Huntington;
Never archer as he so good,
And the people called him Robin Hood.
Such outlaws as he and his men
Will England never see again.

A Final Word

No one — even people who believe there really was a Robin Hood — has ever found that grave. Does this mean there never was a real Robin Hood? Over the years many people have tried, without success, to answer that question. The mystery of Robin Hood remains unsolved.

But fact or fiction, Robin and his men have lived for hundreds of years in some of the best stories ever told. And real or unreal, Robin Hood and his merry men will probably live on in those stories forever.

Whether or not we believe Robin Hood was real, for centuries he has brought comfort to people around the world. Perhaps we find in Robin Hood everything we hope is in ourselves. He was — and is — the kind of hero we would all like to be.